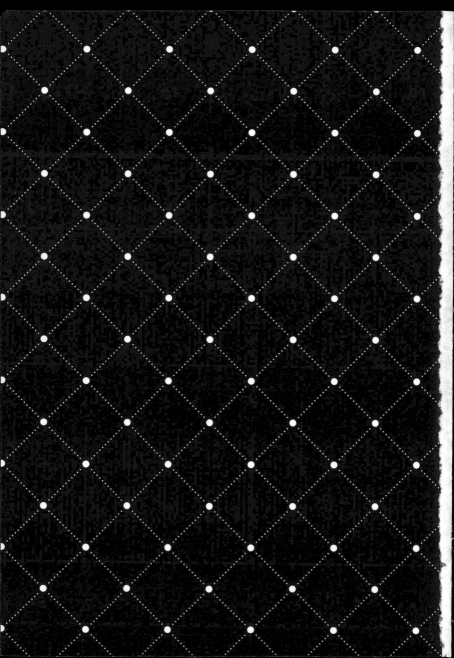

THE WORLD ACCORDING TO

COCO

THE WIT AND WISDOM OF COCO CHANEL

Edited by
Patrick Mauriès
Jean-Christophe Napias

Illustrations and design by
Isabelle Chemin

Thames & Hudson

The World According to Coco © 2020
Thames & Hudson Ltd, London
Edited compilation © 2020 Patrick Mauriès and Jean-Christophe Napias
Foreword © 2020 Patrick Mauriès

All Rights Reserved. No part of this publication
may be reproduced or transmitted in any form or by
any means, electronic or mechanical, including photocopy,
recording or any other information storage and retrieval
system, without prior written permission from the publisher.

Quotations reproduced from Paul Morand's *L'Allure de Chanel* ©
1976, Hermann, www.editions-hermann.fr. Translation taken from
The Allure of Chanel © 2008, Pushkin Press. Additional quotations
reproduced from Louise de Vilmorin's *Mémoires de Coco* © 1999,
Éditions Gallimard. All translations from the French language by
Thames & Hudson unless otherwise stated. Quotations by Karl Lagerfeld
reproduced from *The World According to Karl* © 2013, Karl Lagerfeld.
For full credits see p.174–75.

Illustrations and design by Isabelle Chemin. Illustrations on p.10 & 160
based on photograph © Boris Lipnitzki/Roger-Viollet. Illustration on
p.26 based on illustration © Condé Nast.

The authors and publisher would like to thank Hélène Fulgence and
Cécile Goddet-Dirles of the Patrimoine Chanel for their invaluable help
in the making of this book.

First published in the United States of America by Thames & Hudson
Inc., 500 Fifth Avenue, New York, New York 10110

www.thamesandhudsonusa.com

Library of Congress Control Number 2019954081

ISBN 978-0-500-02348-8

Printed and bound in Italy

CONTENTS

Foreword *Patrick Mauriès* 6

Coco on Coco 11
Coco on Fashion 27
Coco on Couture 41
Coco on Style 57
Coco on Elegance 67
Coco on Jewellery 77
Coco on Fragrance 85
Coco on Colour 95
Coco on Work 103
Coco on Invention 111
Coco on Luxury 119
Coco on Time 129
The Wit of Coco 137
Karl on Coco 153
Coco on Coco 2 161

Sources 174

LA GRANDE MADEMOISELLE

In 1920, at the start of what would be called her Russian period, if she were a painter, Coco Chanel hardly said a word. Accustomed to living in the shadow of her companions, and alone following the premature death of Boy Capel, she happened to make the acquaintance of the effusive Misia Sert and was thus invited into literary and artistic circles that had formerly been unknown or off limits to her. 'Nobody knew her,' wrote Edmonde Charles-Roux. 'She was hardly introduced. Nobody heard her speak. She watched and listened.'

This collection of quotations could be the fruit of that time spent listening. There may seem to be a great distance between the small, slim, silent woman standing beside Misia Sert and the official dictates of the besuited priestess with the square jaw and thin lips, her elocution nonchalant but precise, her scratchy voice lingering in the memory. But it's only the span of a lifetime, and a wealth of experience.

The founding contradiction in Chanel's vision is well known – she herself willingly admitted to it, and Roland Barthes underlined it in his famous essay 'The Contest between Chanel and Courrèges', written in 1967. Having devoted her life to the fickle world of fashion – 'every year fashion destroys that which it has just been admiring, it adores that which it is about to destroy' – she sought only the impermanence of style, an enduring principle, allowing only carefully calculated variations, based on a Platonic idea of idealized (feminine) beauty.

The same quest for style, for the sharpest and neatest formulation, also influenced her conversation, as Barthes rather ironically pointed out: 'She is commonly attributed with the authority and the panache of a writer of the Grand Siècle: elegant like Racine, Jansenist like Pascal (whom she quotes), philosophical like La Rochefoucauld (whom she imitates by delivering her own maxims to the public), sensitive like Madame de Sévigné and, finally, rebellious like the "Grande Mademoiselle" whose nickname and role she borrows.' In this regard, the 'Grande Mademoiselle' was the product of her times: of the culture, the traditions and the rituals of (high) society, to which she was introduced in her early years and which began to fade slowly away from the 1950s onwards, until it finally expired, along with its last surviving members, in the 1970s.

This culture was one that she shared with writers – Louise de Vilmorin, Paul Morand, Edmonde Charles-Roux, Michel Déon – whom she employed one by one, only to sack them after a short while, but who nonetheless managed to record a number of her *bon mots*. We later see the traces of this shared spirit when we hear her speak via Paul Morand's *The Allure of Chanel* (the same love of pithy phrases, the same dryness of wit), which might lead us to believe that her words have been heavily rewritten and polished, but Morand for the most part was content to simply transcribe what he heard: a shared vision, taste, culture and values, for better or sometimes for worse. All that Chanel needed was a mouthpiece, and yet they were never quite to her taste.

A self-proclaimed lover of the 18th century, Karl Lagerfeld is well known for having shared her love of making a splash with a finely honed phrase or a cutting remark, taking it to an even higher degree of topicality and intensity. Less uncompromising, more calculated than Coco, happy to play the media games that she would have loathed, and using his public image as something to hide behind, he was in this respect – as he was in his way of reworking and reinventing her designs – the perfect heir to the Grande Mademoiselle. This made him her ideal interpreter at a time when an all-powerful Fashion was incessantly extending the bounds of its empire, until it took on the economic and cultural significance it now possesses, and which only seems to be growing in strength.

In 1969, Chanel created what was then seen as a scandal by vehemently denouncing the 'immodesty', 'indecency' and 'lack of morals' symbolized by the revealing of bare knees ('an ugly joint') occasioned by the mini skirt. We can hardly dare to imagine her reaction to the carefree exhibitionism, the glorified narcissism, the silicone-enhanced bodies, the mindless selfies and the all-conquering idiocy that characterize our current era. Nothing could be further from what she called style, and from what she believed to be an unchanging, universal and eternal quality. Style itself is nothing but the plaything of history.

Patrick Mauriès

COCO
ON
COCO

I have a few virtues, reasonably charming ones;
I am full of impossible faults.

I hate to demean myself, to submit to anyone, to
humiliate myself, not to speak plainly, to give in,
not to have my own way.

I owe my powerful build to my very tough
upbringing. Yes, pride is the key to my bad temper,
to my gypsy-like independence, to my antisocial
nature; it's the Ariadne's thread that has always
enabled me to find my way back.

I am irritated, irritable and irritating.

I know that I'm unbearable.

Without trying,
**I've always
been**
different
**from other
people.**

I love to criticize;

the day I can no longer criticize, life will be over for me.

*One day, my car was parked quite far from the
pavement. To get out, I had to take a big stride
over the gutter, but I was wearing a tight skirt
and it wasn't easy. Watching my gymnastics, two
workmen sitting by the side of the road burst out
laughing. I decided, from that day onwards, that I
would always be on the side of those who laughed,
and never on the side of those who were laughed at.*

*I hate it when people put their hands on me, as if
I were a cat.*

Do you see what a foul temper I really have?

*I am the only volcano from the region of Auvergne
that isn't extinct.*

I know how to work. I know how to discipline myself. But if I don't want to do something, nothing and nobody can make me do it.

I don't have anyone to discipline me. I discipline myself.

I cannot take orders from anyone else, except in love; and even then...

The one thing that isn't for sale is Mademoiselle Chanel.

I am a bee,

it's part of my star sign, Leo,
the Lion, the sun. Women with this
sign are hard-working, courageous,
faithful, they are not daunted
by anything. That's my personality.
I am a bee born under the
sign of the Lion.

THE MORE PEOPLE CAME TO CALL ON ME,

THE MORE I HID AWAY.

THIS HABIT HAS ALWAYS REMAINED WITH ME.

Every time I've done something reasonable,
it's brought me bad luck.

Audacity and shyness are the two extremes of
my personality.

You must learn to be playful with your faults, to
play tricks with them. If you learn to do this well,
you can achieve anything.

The hardness of the mirror reflects my own
hardness back to me; it's a struggle between it and
me: it expresses what is peculiar to myself, a person
who is efficient, optimistic, passionate, realistic,
combative, mocking and incredulous, and who feels
her Frenchness. Finally, there are my gold-brown
eyes which guard the entrance to my heart: there
one can see that I am a woman.

*Despite the time I have spent searching for myself,
I have not yet arrived at myself, for between us there
is something insurmountable.*

*When my friends tease me for my habit of talking
incessantly, it's because they don't understand that
I'm terrified of being bored listening to other people.
If I die one day, I believe that it will only be from
boredom.*

*Why did I come back? I was getting bored. I spent
fifteen years trying to understand myself. Now I
prefer disaster to nothingness.*

*Boredom has been my life-long enemy. I work so
I won't be bored. I don't do it for money. I don't
do it for women. I see too many of them. And I see
those who do nothing. They do nothing. They are
nothing. They are dead.*

I am
only
FRIGHTENED
of
one
thing:
being
BORED.

I go on
my greatest
journeys
on
my couch.

As for me, I belong to that breed of foolish women, women who think only of their work, and, once work is done, think of fortune-tellers, stories about other people, daily events and nonsense.

I only care for trivial things, or else nothing at all, because that is where poetry takes shelter.

Reality does not make me dream, and I love to dream.

I have always tried to design new dresses that women can wear for many years. Is it arrogant to say that I have succeeded?

I think that I don't love people who don't love me.
It's a great source of protection in life – I know
straight away when people don't love me. I also
know when people don't like me. And that's a very
unpleasant thing. And I don't think anyone else
understands that.

I don't ask people to love me: that's a strong word.
I can't love everyone either. I love very few people
– what people call love, being devoted to someone
body and soul. Love like that is rare.

I have a great disdain for all women, starting with
myself, since I can say without a doubt that nobody
has a worse opinion of me than I do.

I don't
have lukewarm
feelings
about anyone:

I either
like them
♡ OR
I don't.

COCO
ON
FASHION

Fashion? When people ask me what I think of fashion, I don't know what they're talking about... What is fashion? Every now and then, I change a small detail, a neckline, a sleeve – sleeves are so important in a dress – and immediately everything else goes out of fashion… But I only do it so the garment works better. I don't sit around racking my brains, wondering how I'm going to shake everything up!

It is not by learning to make dresses that they become successful (making dresses and creating fashion are different things). Fashion does not exist only in dresses; fashion is in the air, it is borne on the wind, you can sense it, you can breathe it, it's in the sky and on the highway, it's everywhere, it has to do with ideas, with social mores, with events.

I am neither behind the times nor ahead of the times; my fashion follows life.

I would very much like to call a meeting of couturiers and ask them each the same question:

What is fashion? Explain it to me.

I am convinced that none of them could give me a meaningful answer. Neither could I, in fact.

1er Arr^t

A FASHION THAT
NEVER REACHES
THE STREETS IS
NOT A FASHION.

There will be no knees on show in my fashion house. The knee is a joint. Do you think a joint can be beautiful?

I have created fashion for a quarter of a century. Why? Because I knew how to express my times. I invented the sports dress for myself; not because other women played sports, but because I did. I didn't go out because I needed to design dresses, I designed dresses precisely because I went out, because I have lived the life of the century, and was the first to do so.

It's always best to follow fashion, even if it is ugly. To distance oneself from it is immediately to become a comical character, which is terrifying. No one is powerful enough to be more powerful than fashion.

Fashion moves forwards, not backwards – there's no going back. You must live with the times…

A dress or a suit must always reflect today, like a perfume lingering in the air, a perfume that says: I have passed by and I am still here.

Fashion is the only thing that grows old very fast – much faster than a woman does.

To me, fashion is not fun, it's something that verges on suicide.

In matters of fashion too, it's only imbeciles who never change their minds.

The best proof that fashion is not made to be preserved is that it goes out of fashion. And quickly, too!

FASHION WANTS TO BE KILLED IT IS DESIGNED FOR THAT.

*I have created fashion for a quarter of a century.
Why? Because I knew how to express my times. I
invented the sports dress for myself; not because other
women played sports, but because I did. I didn't go out
because I needed to design dresses, I designed dresses
precisely because I went out, because I have lived the
life of the century, and was the first to do so.*

*It's always best to follow fashion, even if it is ugly.
To distance oneself from it is immediately to become
a comical character, which is terrifying. No one is
powerful enough to be more powerful than fashion.*

*Fashion moves forwards, not backwards – there's
no going back. You must live with the times...*

A dress or a suit must always reflect today, like a perfume lingering in the air, a perfume that says: I have passed by and I am still here.

Fashion is the only thing that grows old very fast – much faster than a woman does.

To me, fashion is not fun, it's something that verges on suicide.

In matters of fashion too, it's only imbeciles who never change their minds.

The best proof that fashion is not made to be preserved is that it goes out of fashion. And quickly, too!

FASHION WANTS TO BE KILLED; IT IS DESIGNED FOR THAT.

There will be no knees on show in my fashion house. The knee is a joint. Do you think a joint can be beautiful?

Newness! You can't always be doing something new!

The absurd notion that fashion depends on the length of the skirt: short today, long tomorrow... Fashion, of course, is a matter of taste, good taste, and the length of a skirt depends on the legs. If they are good, show them. If not, don't. Simple, isn't it – or should I say sensible?

Fashion is a serious thing. I don't think fashion should aim to constantly shock. You can't just demolish everything that you've built, once or twice a year.

I am against the absurdity of creating fashion that does not last... To me, old clothes are like old friends, you know? You take care of your clothes. You repair them.

There are no intelligent women at a couturier's.
(Nor moral women; they would sell their soul
for a dress.)

Look at those women working in the press who
decide what is in fashion. They are fat, ugly and
badly dressed!

I do not want a woman to dress like a man.
As soon as a woman starts dressing like a man
and behaving like a man, she is lost.

I hate
it when women
follow fashion too

BLINDLY,

at the expense
of their
personalities.

What we
create in
fashion
should first be
beautiful
and then
become
ugly;
what art
creates should
first be
ugly
and then
become
beautiful.

*Fashion should be discussed enthusiastically and
sanely; and above all without poetry, without
literature. A dress is neither a tragedy nor a
painting; it is a charming and ephemeral creation,
not an everlasting work of art. Fashion should
die and die quickly, in order that commerce
may survive.*

*I am a little scared when I see friends of French
fashion behave with so much respect towards it.
Is it my familiarity with it that lets me treat it as
a living and perishable thing, and not as an eternal
testimony to genius? I don't know.*

*For fashion roams around the streets, unaware that
it exists, up to the moment that I, in my own way,
may have expressed it. Fashion, like landscape, is
a state of mind, by which I mean my own.*

COCO
ON
COUTURE

*Couture is a business, not an art. We aren't
geniuses, we are suppliers. We don't hang our
garments on the wall to exhibit them, we sell them.*

*Costume designers work with a pencil: it's an art.
Couturiers work with scissors and pins: it's a
news bulletin.*

*Couture is not an abstract art but a craft, and it
is about form in the truest sense of the word. It is
the form of the garment that counts. And the form
of the woman inside it. A woman is more than two
knees. Thankfully.*

I DON'T KNOW
how to
SEW,
I know
WHERE TO
PUT PINS.

I NEED
beautiful
models.
THERE ARE SOME
GIRLS I COULD
NEVER WORK WITH,
right pains
in the neck.

*I work directly on the body. I draw inspiration from
my models, not from my drawings. That is why
I change models so often. I work with a pair of
scissors and lots of pins.*

*The reign of the model-as-object needs to end.
My models are real women, not apparitions.*

*A model is like a watch. A watch reveals the time.
A model must reveal the dress she's wearing.*

*I could not wear something that I would not
also make. And I could not make something that
I would not wear. I always ask myself the
same question: in all honesty, would I wear that?
I actually don't even need to ask any more, it
has become an instinct.*

*Fashion is architecture, a matter of proportions
above all else. The hardest thing to make would be
a well-proportioned dress that suits every woman,
a dress that five different women could wear without
people immediately realizing that it's the same one.*

*Were I writing a technical handbook, I would say
to you: 'A well-made dress suits everyone.'*

All   the artistry
that's needed
underneath   to
make a
dress   move
well.

That's what
fashion is:

what's   happening

underneath.

A dress that isn't comfortable is a failure.

Some women want to be corseted in their clothes.
Never! I want women to step into my dresses and
not give a damn about the rest.

A Chanel suit is built for a woman who moves.

Clothes should be as mobile as the woman
who wears them.

For a suit to be pretty, the woman wearing
it must appear naked underneath.

Suits are a question of construction. And people call them 'little Chanel suits'…

Perfection should be found where you least expect it.

Nothing should be pointless, everything must have a function: no button without a buttonhole.

Why do you want to keep all of that on there? Cut it off and be done with it.

Do the lines of an aeroplane have frills? No. I created my collection thinking about planes.

No one should be frightened of pleats: a pleat is always beautiful if it is useful…

THE ONLY LINE IS THE STRAIGHT LINE.

I NEVER
FINISH
A DRESS.

I keep working on them
until the very last day.
Sometimes until the night
before a show.

Out of fear that they
will go out of fashion.

I STRIP
THEM
AND STRIP THEM,

taking away everything I've
added that I feel is superfluous.

A fine fabric is beautiful in itself, but the more lavish a dress is, the poorer it becomes.

Fantasy gowns? I know how to make those too...
You always start by making a dream gown.
And then you have to take them apart, trim them
down, take bits off. Always take away. Never add.

Right up to the last day, I'm making changes.
What do you expect? I make my dresses on
the models.

Couture is my joy, my goal, my ideal, my raison
d'être, *my everything, my self... I am nothing*
but a little seamstress.

I was the one who made couturiers fashionable. Before me, they weren't in the slightest.

People aren't excited by fashion itself, but by the people who make it. People always get everything mixed up.

Nowadays, people who work in couture think only about trying to shock. Who?

If haute couture was only about skirt length, then any maid who can sew could become a couturier. All that would be left for us to do would be to go to the cinema or watch television.

COUTURIERS
Think themselves
to be so
IMPORTANT

...

COCO
ON
STYLE

I don't like it when people talk about Chanel as a fashion. Chanel is a style, first and foremost. Fashion goes out of fashion. Style never.

Other designers pursued fashion, whereas I created a style.

That's why I created a style: I could never cope if I had to come up with something new every week. It's not possible. You'd end up creating very ugly things.

I AM A
SLAVE TO MY
OWN STYLE.

A STYLE
NEVER GOES
OUT OF FASHION.

CHANEL
NEVER GOES
OUT OF
FASHION.

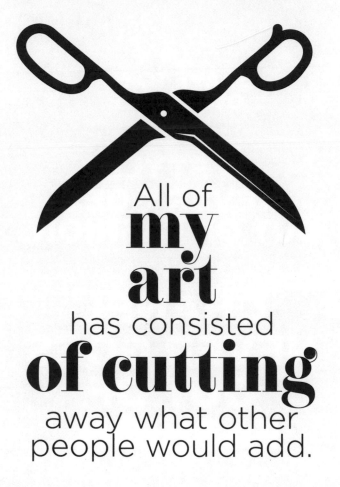

All of
my
art
has consisted
of cutting
away what other
people would add.

*Style should reach the people, no? It should
descend into the streets, into people's lives, like
a revolution. That is real style. The rest is fashion.
Fashion passes; style remains. Fashion consists of a
few amusing ideas, meant to be used up quickly.*

*Always take away, always pare back. Never add...
There is no beauty except the freedom of the body...*

*Streamline a woman from head to toe; because
in doing this you make her more youthful.*

*I think that my clothes, famous for their simplicity,
haven't been simple enough so far. I will make them
even simpler.*

Simplicity does not mean poverty.

Style is more than that. It's the cut. It's the proportions, the colours, the fabrics. And more than that – more than anything – it's the woman herself.

What is the most difficult part of my job? Allowing women to move easily, so that they don't feel as if they're wearing fancy dress. So they don't have to change their attitude or their personality to suit the dress that they've been stuffed into. It's very difficult, but that's the talent I possess, if you can call it a talent.

Dress a woman for today and you will also dress her for tomorrow. That's the paradox of style.

IT'S THE
LITTLE
THINGS
THAT ARE
IMPORTANT
IN LIFE,

NOT THE BIG THINGS.

I don't like

ECCENTRICITY

except in
others.

Clothes should never be funny, even when they are eccentric. Making people laugh at the way you look means being ridiculous. Having a unique style and astounding people with an elegance whose discretion and effects defy analysis, that's what a woman should aim for if she wants to retain her mystery and have an air of poetry.

An elegant woman should be able to do her groceries without making the housewives laugh. The ones who laugh are always in the right.

One must beware of originality; in dressmaking, you immediately descend to disguise and decoration, you lapse into stage design.

I never do anything ridiculous. I detest ridiculousness. It's not my style. I've found my own style, for once and for all, and I'm sticking to it.

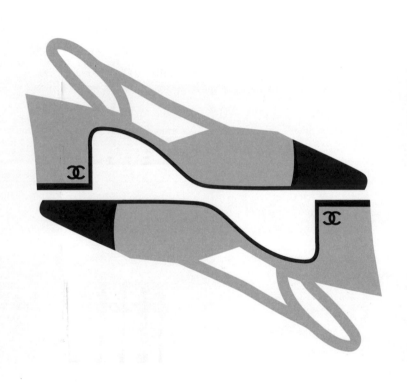

COCO
ON
ELEGANCE

Define elegance? My God, that's difficult… I can only tell you what I always say, and which I believe is true: I think that women are always overdressed but never elegant enough.

You don't need to wear Chanel to be elegant. It would be very unfortunate if it were necessary to wear Chanel in order to be elegant.

Elegance does not lie in mimicry, but in the instinct that directs a woman towards what suits her body and her personality.

Always be a
little
underdressed
rather than
a little
overdressed.

Elegance
is line.

*A touch of beauty or elegance has the same
fantastical power as a candle flame in a dark room.*

*Elegance is not the prerogative of those who
are barely adults, but of women who have found
their equilibrium, their personality. They don't need
money, they already possess a richness of the heart
– and elegance.*

*Elegance? It is not a question of money.
It is the antithesis of vulgarity and sloppiness.
You can be overdressed, but you can never be too
elegant. If you are ugly, people will eventually
overlook it. But never if you are sloppy.*

What is elegance? A way of standing, walking, sitting. Not just dressing. You must be able to please people without anything else, by your presence alone.

A woman is almost more naked when she is well dressed.

Don't think that elegance can be bought with money, affection or imitation. Your dresses and jewellery should belong to you as much as your gestures, your walk or your smile. This is the only way that they can make you beautiful without disguising you. The words of Beau Brummell are still true: 'elegance goes unnoticed'.

It is not **the dress** that should wear **the woman**, but **the woman** who should wear **the dress.**

Hide what you ought to show; show what you cannot *hide*.

The chic of a dress does not lie in its concept, but in the fine quality of the fabric, the cut, and the execution of its idea. It's always better to have two perfect dresses than four mediocre ones.

Elegance does not mean buying a new dress. You're not elegant because you have a new dress. You're elegant because you're elegant. There are some people who don't have it and never will.

COCO
ON
JEWELLERY

I readily wear a lot of jewellery because, on me, it always looks artificial.

When I have time, I take a box of wax and I mould something with my hands. This is also how I make my jewellery. Proportion is what counts.

Jewellery is not meant to make you look rich, but to make you look adorned – it's not the same thing.

Jewellery
is never anything
but a reflection
of the
heart.

The problem that
needs to be solved
when making
FAKE
jewellery
is how to make
it seem more
REAL
than the
REAL thing.

*Jewellery should be looked upon innocently,
naively, rather as one enjoys the sight of an apple
tree in blossom by the side of the road, as one
speeds by in a motor car.*

*The point of jewellery is to pay respect to those for
whom, and at whose homes, one wears it.*

*Jewellery is not meant to arouse envy;
still less astonishment. It should remain an
ornament and an amusement.*

*Once, jewellery began life as designs… My jewels
represent an idea first and foremost! I wanted
to cover women in constellations. Stars! Stars of
all sizes, sparkling in their hair, their fringes,
crescent moons.*

*My jewellery is never separate from the idea of
a woman and her dress. It's because the dresses
change that my jewellery changes too.*

What counts are not the carats, but the illusion.

N°5

COCO
ON
FRAGRANCE

I wanted to create a perfume for women, but a perfume that is artificial like a dress: something fabricated. I am a craftswoman of couture. I don't want rose or lily of the valley, I want a perfume that is a compound.

Perfume? Nothing is more important... What is essential is that it resembles the person who wears it... A badly perfumed woman is one who doesn't wear perfume at all, who is so haughty that she thinks her own natural scent is enough. Well, it isn't!

I have been
a couturier,
by
chance.

I have made
perfumes,
by
chance.

Where should you put perfume?

66 *Everywhere you want to be kissed.*

What do
you eat?

"A gardenia
in the morning
and a rose
in the evening.

A perfume should
hit you.
I'm not going to spend
three days sniffing to
find out what it smells
like, you know?

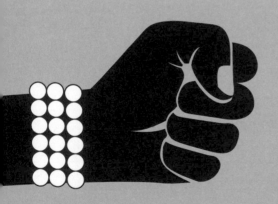

It needs to have a body,
and the things that give
perfume a body are the
most expensive.

A woman who says 'I never wear perfume', and whose coat smells like a wardrobe has already lost. She's setting out in life without a chance.

Women wear the perfumes they are given! But equally you should wear a perfume you love, one that belongs to you. When I leave a jacket behind somewhere, people know that it belongs to me.

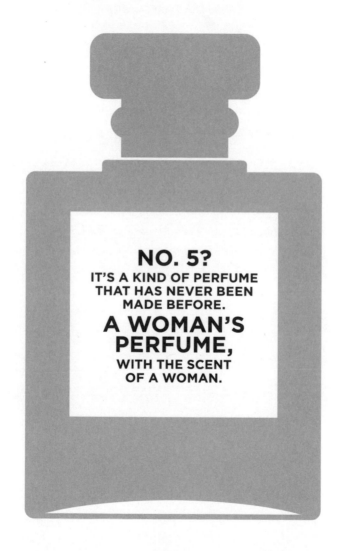

NO. 5?
IT'S A KIND OF PERFUME
THAT HAS NEVER BEEN
MADE BEFORE.
**A WOMAN'S
PERFUME,**
WITH THE SCENT
OF A WOMAN.

NO. 5 NEVER GOES 'OFF'.
IF YOU LIKE NO. 5, DO WHAT I DO, AND STAY FAITHFUL TO IT. IT'S AN EASY WAY TO BE YOURSELF, AND NOT SOMEONE ELSE.

COCO
ON
COLOUR

I asked wholesalers for natural colours; I wanted women to be guided by nature, to obey the mimicry of animals. A green dress on a lawn is perfectly acceptable.

I take refuge in beige, because it's natural. Undyed. And red, because it's the colour of blood and we have so much inside of us that we ought to show a little of it on the outside.

RED

IS THE COLOUR OF

LIFE,

OF BLOOD.

I LOVE

RED.

Before ME, nobody dared to wear BLACK.

*So I imposed black; it's still going strong today,
for black wipes out everything else around.*

*For four or five years, I only used black. My dresses
sold like hot cakes. I gave them a small added
touch, a little white collar or cuffs. Everybody
wore them: from actresses and society ladies to
chambermaids.*

*Women think of every colour, except the absence
of colours. I have said that black had everything.
White too. They have an absolute beauty. It is
perfect harmony. Dress women in white or black
at a ball: they are the only ones you see.*

*When a well-dressed woman wears a bright colour
(and one that suits her) in the street, the crowds
part before her. They let her walk by; they
admire her.*

*A woman dressed in light colours is rarely in
a bad mood.*

*One day I learned that white, the colour of the
moon, is a symbolic reflection of the absolute.
White is not only an emblem of purity but also
of justice and of its ultimate victory. The robes of
the chosen in the Book of Revelation are white.
White is also the colour of cold, of despair and
of surrender.*

The tragedy

of the ageing woman is that she suddenly remembers that light blue suited her when she was twenty.

COCO
ON
WORK

I have made dresses. I could easily have done something else. It was an accident. I didn't like dresses, but I liked work. I have sacrificed everything to it, even love. Work has consumed my life.

'Everything Coco touches, she transforms into gold', my friends say. The secret of this success is that I have worked terribly hard. I have worked for fifty years, as much as and more than anyone. Nothing can replace work, not securities, or nerve, or luck.

When my business had a life, it was my life; when it had a face, it was my face; when it had a voice, it was my voice; and when I felt that my work loved me, obeyed me and responded to me, I gave myself to it completely. Since then I have had no greater love.

WORK

HAS A

MUCH STRONGER

FLAVOUR

THAN

MONEY.

The word
VACATION
makes me
sweat.

Nothing relaxes me so much as work, and nothing tires me as much as doing nothing. The more I work, the more I want to work.

People want gentleness. But you can't work with gentleness: it isn't real. A hen laying eggs, perhaps. You need anger to work.

What would I do if I didn't work any more? I would get extremely bored.

I only like what I create and I only create if I forget.

It is artists who have taught me rigour.

*I am not an artist. The work of an artist seems
ridiculous at first and then becomes a success.
My work needs to be a success straight away
and to become ridiculous later.*

*I'm always fine-tuning my work; it's like an illness.
I'm doing a job that nobody understands any more.*

*Genius is something you're born with. Talent
is something that needs to be brought out.*

A worker.
I am a
worker.
There are
people who
don't like
that word,
but I'm not
one of them.

COCO
ON
INVENTION

*Once an invention has been revealed, it is destined
for anonymity. I would be unable to exploit
all my ideas, and it's a great pleasure to me to
discover them realized by others, sometimes more
successfully than me.*

*Few designers have been imitated more than
I have. I am on the side of the majority. I think style
should go out into the streets, into daily life, like
a revolution. That's real style.*

Discoveries are made to be lost.

At the beginning of creation,
there is invention.

Invention

is the seed, it's the germ.
For the plant to grow,
you need the right temperature;
that temperature is

luxury.

Fashion should be born
from luxury.

WHEN I AM NO LONGER CREATING, MY LIFE WILL BE OVER.

By starting out with what is beautiful, you can always revert to what is simple, practical and cheap; from a finely made dress, revert to a ready-made. But the opposite is not true. That is why, when you go out into the streets, fashion dies its natural death.

It's out of our power to prevent people from borrowing our ideas sooner or later, provided, of course, that they don't borrow our names or logos.

What nobody can ever steal is authenticity, the spirit of inventiveness, and the perfection of production that is so expensive because it does not emerge from the motor of a sewing machine, but from the hands and mind of a French seamstress.

Those capable of inventing are rare; those who do not invent are many. Therefore, they are stronger.

❧

A failed innovation is painful; a revival of it is sinister.

❧

You can imitate simplicity, but not copy it. Simplicity is perfection.

THE STREET

interests me more
than the salons.

COCO
ON
LUXURY

SOME BELIEVE
THAT
LUXURY
IS THE OPPOSITE
OF POVERTY.

No.

IT IS THE
OPPOSITE OF
VULGARITY.

Luxury is first and foremost the genius of the artist capable of conceiving it and giving it form. This form is then expressed, translated and disseminated by millions of women who conform to it.

To me, luxury is about having well-made clothes, and to be able to wear a suit for five years because it still looks good. That's my dream: vintage suits, used things.

Luxury is a coat that a woman throws over an armchair, inside out... and the inside is more beautiful than the outside.

I have lived in luxury and off luxury, trying to give my contemporaries the exact sense of what it means to me, repeatedly telling them that something only becomes luxurious at the moment when one could, strictly speaking, do without it, but one chooses not to. Luxury is a relaxation of the soul. It satisfies an even deeper aspiration than the need to act or the need to think. One can only compare it to the need to love. Being able to love what is simple is a great luxury.

Luxury should remain almost invisible. It should be felt: a woman who feels enveloped in luxury has a glow.

When the house of Chanel no longer exists, when I am gone, luxury will disappear with me.

LUXURY
CANNOT
BE
COPIED.

It is because it is
**AN ACCURSED
THING**
that

MONEY

should be squandered.

*When rich people spend their money, that's fine.
In any case, rich people and people with money are
not the same thing. Those who have money spend
it, as I have done.*

*I love buying. The dreadful thing is that once you
have bought, you possess.*

*There are people who are made poor by saving
money, and others who grow richer by spending it:
I have always been as poor as Croesus and as rich
as Job.*

I judge people according to the way they spend.

I have never socialized with rich people. Some are so very ordinary, and I would prefer to eat with a tramp than with them, who bore me to death.

I do not like money and, consequently, I do not like people simply because they have money. People who talk about nothing but money are tiresome.

Frugal richness, pretentious opulence, sordid generosity: these are the surest weapons of wealth's suicide.

Money has never been anything to me but the sound of freedom.

Money is not beautiful. It's convenient.

COCO
ON
TIME

*My age depends on the day and the people
I'm with.*

*I am a thousand years old when I am bored,
but when I'm enjoying the company of a friend,
why would I worry about my age?*

*For thirty years, women came to me, young and
old, in order to become more youthful, or, more
precisely, to do what I do: to wear my age well,
which has never been a question of years.*

*I've lived such a full life, I've always chased
after time.*

WANTING
TO GET
YOUNGER:
THAT IS ALREADY
OLD AGE.

Nature gives you your
face at the age of

20

life shapes your face
at the age of

30

but at the age of

50

you have to deserve your face.

The real problem, the greatest one of all, is to make women younger. To make them seem youthful. Stop this and their way of seeing life changes. They become much more cheerful.

Age does not matter: you can be ravishing at twenty, charming at forty and irresistible for the rest of your life.

A woman who is getting older takes more and more care of herself with every passing day; and one of the world's diabolical injustices is that taking care of oneself is what ages one most.

Beauty treatments should begin with the heart and the soul, otherwise cosmetics are pointless.

What does that mean, a 'young fashion'? Dressing like a little girl? There's nothing quite so stupid, nothing that ages you more. People get everything mixed up. Fashion is silly sometimes; people forget that.

A fashion for the young? That's a tautology: there's no fashion for the old.

Love autumn as you would love your own autumn if it finally came and it no longer scared you.

DO YOU THINK IT'S FUN TO CONSTANTLY HEAR PEOPLE SAYING THAT YOU'RE NOT TWENTY ANYMORE?

YOU'RE NOT TWENTY ANY MORE

YOU'RE NOT TWENTY ANY MORE

YOU'RE NOT TWENTY ANY MORE

YOU'RE NOT TWENTY ANY MORE

YOU'RE NOT TWENTY ANY MORE

YOU'RE NOT TWENTY ANY MORE

YOU'RE NOT TWENTY ANY MORE

YOU'RE NOT TWENTY ANY MORE

YOU'RE NOT TWENTY ANY MORE

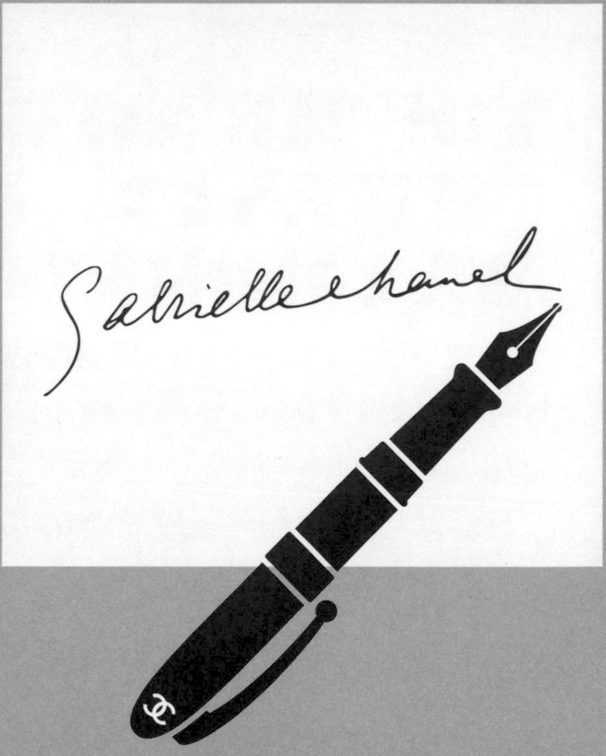
Gabrielle Chanel

THE WIT
OF
COCO

Fashion is always a reflection of the times, but it is forgotten if it is stupid.

Dressing up is delightful; wearing a disguise is sad.

Fashion is a queen and sometimes a slave.

Fashion is both a caterpillar and a butterfly. Be a caterpillar by day and a butterfly by night. There's nothing more comfortable than a caterpillar and there's nothing more made for love than a butterfly. You need dresses that crawl and dresses that fly. The butterfly does not go to the market and the caterpillar does not go to the ball.

Fashion is not theatre, it's the opposite.

THE
POETRY
OF FASHION
IS CREATING AN
ILLUSION.

ADORNMENT,
what a science!

BEAUTY,
what a weapon!

MODESTY,
what elegance!

Make the dress first, not the trimmings.

A dress is not a bandage. It's made to be worn. You wear it with your shoulders. A dress should hang from the shoulders.

Luxury is a necessity that begins where necessity ends.

Nobody, not a designer, not a make-up artist, not even money, can give you charm. Charm is inside you. The trick is discovering it for yourself.

Women can give everything with a smile, and, with a tear, take it all away.

Flirtation is a conquest of the mind over the senses.

True generosity means accepting ingratitude.

You can be loved despite your greatest faults, but hated for your best qualities or greatest virtues.

**If you
were born
WITHOUT
WINGS,**
do not do anything
to stop them from
growing.

You can grow
accustomed to
ugliness;
to
sloppiness,
never.

The only gates you can open are the ones that you have closed yourself.

People only call women sublime in situations of adversity. It is a commonly held belief that allows men to thank them only during catastrophes.

Giving women back their mystery means giving them back their youth.

'Good taste' ruins some of the best qualities of the mind. Taste itself, for example.

There comes a moment when a work cannot be touched any more: that's when it's at its worst.

The smallest real misfortune makes all the misfortunes you imagine disappear.

One can be reduced to infidelity through an excess of delicacy in love.

Since it is agreed that the eyes are the windows of the soul, why do we not admit that the mouth is the gateway to the heart?

You must fashion your life by thinking that everything you do not like has an opposite that you will probably love.

Silences separate more than distance.

Our closest enemies are within us. Those of you who are young, remember that your character traits only teach us their lessons when it is too late.

WHEN YOU NO
LONGER WEEP,
IT'S BECAUSE
YOU NO LONGER
BELIEVE IN
HAPPINESS.

TO BE
irreplaceable,

YOU HAVE
to be
different.

A saint in the world is no more useful than a saint in the desert. If the saints who live in the desert are useless, the ones who live in the world are often dangerous.

Nonchalance is a womanly quality. It is intolerable in a man unless he is a genius.

People do not seek vengeance for their wit or their honour, but for their vanity.

Stupidity is worse than anything... One can forgive everything except stupidity.

KARL
ON
COCO

Chanel's success was knowing how to get across the elements of her identity. Timeless music built around five notes by which women instantly recognize the essence of Chanel: luxury and refinement.

In the 1930s she was much better known for her lace dresses than for her suits. If you say lace, I think of Chanel. Lace: 'dentelle', Chanel… it rhymes.

She invented something: she invented the 'total look'. She was the first to want a 'woman's perfume with a woman's scent', for herself alone. Jewels for her collection. From hats to shoes, from chain-belts to camellias, from bows to bags, she transformed the accessory; she turned the trivial into the essential.

Chanel's style is an

EGO TRIP.

**She did everything
for herself. To assert herself.**

I juggle with what I know and what I don't know about her.

My favourite Coco Chanel is the one at the beginning. The rebellious one, the whimsical one, who cut her hair one evening before a first night at the opera, because a water heater blew up and singed her superb hair. I love her wickedness when she was funny, her intelligence. It's her I think about when I'm designing my collections.

Chanel was a woman of her times. She wasn't a backward-looking has-been. The opposite – she hated the past, including her own past, and her whole thing comes from that. That's why the Chanel brand has to be the image of the moment.

What I've done, Coco Chanel would never have done. She would have hated it.

Chanel is a look that can be adapted to every era, to every age range. It's the elements of a wardrobe, like jeans, the T-shirt, the white shirt. The Chanel jacket is like the two-button suit for a man.

Mademoiselle's genius is to have introduced the suit, the camellia or the gold chain as though she'd invented them. A bit like Charlie Chaplin with his walking stick, his moustache and his hat.

My job is not merely to preserve the Chanel suit, but to keep it alive.

I adore Chanel, but it is not me.

I KNOW CHANEL'S DNA THOROUGHLY,

and it's strong enough not to have to talk about it.

COCO
ON
COCO
2

When I was young, women did not have a form.
I gave them back their freedom: I gave them real
arms, real legs, proper movement, the ability to
laugh and eat without discomfort.

I wonder why I embarked upon this profession,
and why I'm thought of as a revolutionary figure?
It was not in order to create what I liked, but
rather to make what I disliked unfashionable.
I have used my talent like an explosive.

I was working for a new society. Until then, fashion
had been for useless, idle women, who needed
chambermaids to pass their stockings; now I had
a clientele of active women, and an active woman
needs to feel at ease in her clothes. She needs to be
able to roll up her sleeves.

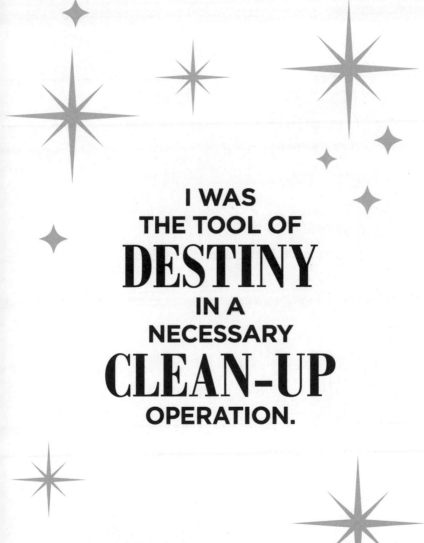

I WAS
THE TOOL OF
DESTINY
IN A
NECESSARY
CLEAN-UP
OPERATION.

One world was ending,
another was about to be
born. I was in the right
place; an opportunity
beckoned, I took it.

I had grown up with this new century: I was therefore the one to be consulted about its sartorial style. What were needed were simplicity, comfort and neatness: unwittingly, I offered all of that. True success is inevitable.

People always wanted to put me in a cage: cages with pillows stuffed with promises, golden cages, cages that I touched with one finger and then turned away from. I never wanted any cage other than the one I could build for myself.

*At the age of barely twenty, I founded a couture
house. It was not the creation of an artist, as
it has become common to claim, or that of a
businesswoman, but the work of a creature seeking
nothing but freedom.*

*I have given women's bodies back their freedom;
that body perspired in formal clothing, beneath the
lacework, the corsets, the underwear, the padding.*

*I want women to be pretty. And free. Free to swing
their arms and move quickly. With the times.*

Luck
is a way
of being.

Luck
is not a
little person.

Luck
is my
soul.

*Luck is a delicate thing. I arrived at the right
moment and I met the people I needed to know.*

*It irritates me when I hear people say that I've been
lucky. No one has worked harder than me.*

*I tend to consider my success as a proof of love, and I
want to believe that by loving what I was doing, I was
loved in return through my creations.*

*It is loneliness that has forged my character, which is
bad-tempered, and bronzed my soul, which is proud,
and my body, which is sturdy.*

People think that all the doors were opened in front of me, but it was me who pushed them open...

This is what celebrity is: solitude.

COCO ON COCO 2

My life is the story – and often the tragedy – of the solitary woman, her woes, her importance, the unequal and fascinating battle she has waged with herself, with men, and with the attractions, the weaknesses and the dangers that spring up everywhere.

I have a horror of loneliness and I live in total solitude. I would pay so as not to be alone.

There is nothing worse than being alone. No, there is something: being alone in a couple.

I no longer know whether I have been happy. I'm curious about one thing: death.

All I aspire to is tranquillity. I hope they'll let me rest in peace after my death.

Chanel clients read luxury magazines: Vogue, Harper's Bazaar. *These magazines do our advertising. Popular magazines, with big print runs, are even better. They create our legend.*

Legend is the consecration of celebrity.

People who have a legend become that legend too.

This is all a joke; I tell you jokes because I don't want to tell you about myself. I'm not an important enough person.

I'm not
going to tell
you my entire
life story!

SOURCES

BOOKS

Danièle Bott, *Chanel* (Paris: Ramsay, 2005) • Edmonde Charles-Roux, *L'Irrégulière ou mon itinéraire Chanel* (Paris: Grasset, 1974) • Edmonde Charles-Roux, *Le Temps Chanel* (Paris: Éditions de La Martinière/Grasset, 2004) • Claude Delay, *Chanel solitaire* (Paris: Gallimard, 1983) • Pierre Galante, *Les Années Chanel* (Paris-Match/Mercure de France, 1972) • Marcel Haedrich, *Coco Chanel secrète* (Paris: Belfond, 1971) • Lilou Marquand, *Chanel m'a dit* (Paris: JC Lattès, 1990) • Patrick Mauriès, Jean-Christophe Napias and Sandrine Gulbenkian, *The World According to Karl: The Wit and Wisdom of Karl Lagerfeld* (London: Thames & Hudson, 2013) • Paul Morand, *L'Allure de Chanel* (Paris: Hermann, 1976) • Louise de Vilmorin, *Mémoires de Coco* (Paris: Éditions Gallimard, 1999)

MAGAZINES AND NEWSPAPERS

Elle • Figaro Magazine • Harper's Bazaar US • La Revue des sports et du monde • Le Nouveau Femina • L'Express • L'Illustré de Lausanne • L'Intransigeant • Le Point • Marianne • Marie Claire • McCall's • Mirabella • Paris Match • Série Limitée • Stiletto • The New Yorker • Time • Town and Country • Vogue France

INTERVIEWS

Interview with Pierre Dumayet (from the programme *Cinq Colonnes à la Une*, 1959) • Interviews with Jacques Chazot (from the programme *DIM DAM DOM* 11th February, 1968 and a television news broadcast from 30th January, 1970) • CD *Coco Chanel Parle. La Mode Qu'est-ce que c'est ?* (from the 'Français de notre temps' series, 1972) • France 3 • CNN

The following quotations are taken from *Mémoires de Coco* by Louise de Vilmorin (Éditions Gallimard, 1999): p.19, 'Audacity and shyness are…' • p.58, 'Other designers pursued fashion…' • p.65, 'Clothes should never be funny…' • p.100, 'One day I learned that white…' • p.104, 'When my business had a life…' • p.162, 'When I was young, women did not…' • p.165, 'People always wanted to put me in a cage…' • p.166, 'At the age of barely twenty…' • p.168, 'I tend to consider my success…'

The following quotations are taken from *L'Allure de Chanel* by Paul Morand (trans. Pushkin Press, 2008): p.12, 'I have a few virtues, reasonably charming…' • p.12, 'I hate to demean myself…' • p.12, 'I owe my powerful build to…' • p.12, 'I am irritated, irritable…' • p.13, 'Without trying...' • p.14, 'I love to criticize…' • p.15, 'Do you see what a foul temper…' • p.16, 'I cannot take orders from…' • p.18, 'The more people came to call…' • p.19, 'Every time I've done something…' • p.19, 'The hardness of the mirror…' • p.23, 'As for me, I belong to that breed…' • p.23, 'I only care for trivial things…' • p.23, 'I only like what I create…' • p.28, 'It is not by learning…' • p.31, 'I have created fashion…' • p.31, 'It's best to follow fashion…' • p.33, 'Fashion wants to be killed…' • p.36, 'There are no intelligent women…' • p.39, 'Fashion should be discussed…' • p.39, 'For fashion roams around the…' • p.46, 'Were I writing a technical …' • p.50, 'No one should be frightened of pleats…' • p.53, 'A fine fabric is beautiful in itself…' • p.64, 'I don't like eccentricity…' • p.65, 'One must beware of originality…' • p.78, 'I readily wear a lot of…' • p.78, 'When I have time...' • p.78, 'Jewellery is not to make you look….' • p.87, 'I have been a couturier…' • p.96, 'I asked wholesalers for natural colours…' • p.99, 'So I imposed black...' • p.99, 'Women think of every colour…' • p.101, 'The tragedy of the ageing…' • p.104, 'I have made dresses…' • p.104, 'Everything Coco touches…' • p.105, 'Work has a much…' • p.107, 'Nothing relaxes me so much as…' • p.112, 'Once an invention has...' • p.113, 'At the beginning of creation...' • p.115, 'By starting out with...' • p.121, 'Luxury is first and foremost…' • p.124, 'It is because it is an accursed thing…' • p.125, 'I judge people according to…' • p.125, 'I love buying…' • p.133, 'A woman who is getting older...' • p.133, 'Beauty treatments should…' • p.162, 'I wonder why I embarked…' • p.164, 'One world was ending…' • p.165, 'I had grown up with this new century…' • p.166, 'I have given women's bodies back…' • p.168, 'It irritates me when I hear…' • p.168, 'It is loneliness that has…' • p.171, 'My life is the story – and often the…' • p.171, 'I have a horror of loneliness…'

ABOUT THE AUTHORS

A writer, editor and journalist, Patrick Mauriès has published numerous books and essays on art, literature, fashion and the decorative arts. He has written books on a range of figures including Jean-Paul Goude, Christian Lacroix and Karl Lagerfeld.

Jean-Christophe Napias is an author, publisher and editor. He is the author of several books on Paris (including *Quiet Corners of Paris*) and has edited works on French literature.

Patrick Mauriès and Jean-Christophe Napias have previously co-authored titles including *The World According to Karl*, *Choupette: The Private Life of a High-Flying Fashion Cat* and *Fashion Quotes*.

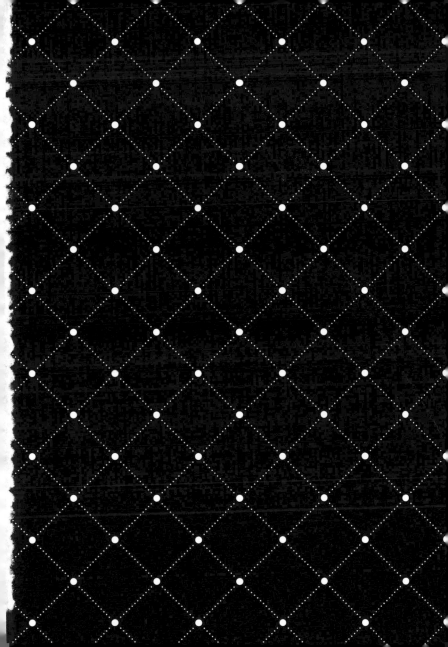

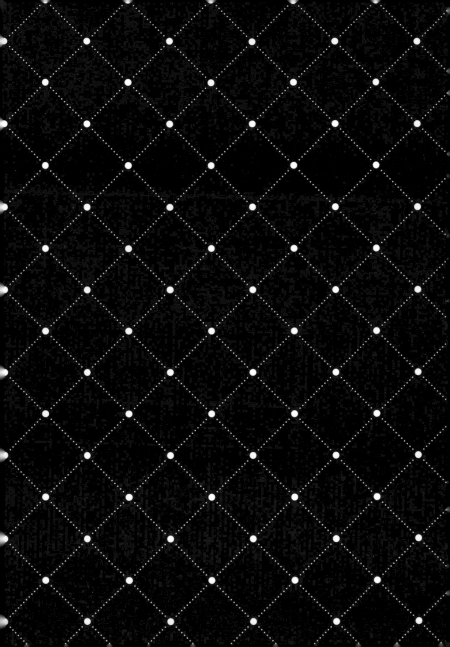